CELEBRATING HOLIDAYS

Earth Day

by Rachel Grack

BELLWETHER MEDIA • MINNEAPOLIS, MN

Note to Librarians, Teachers, and Parents:

Blastoff! Readers are carefully developed by literacy experts and combine standards-based content with developmentally appropriate text.

Level 1 provides the most support through repetition of high-frequency words, light text, predictable sentence patterns, and strong visual support.

Level 2 offers early readers a bit more challenge through varied simple sentences, increased text load, and less repetition of high-frequency words.

Level 3 advances early-fluent readers toward fluency through increased text and concept load, less reliance on visuals, longer sentences, and more literary language.

Level 4 builds reading stamina by providing more text per page, increased use of punctuation, greater variation in sentence patterns, and increasingly challenging vocabulary.

Level 5 encourages children to move from "learning to read" to "reading to learn" by providing even more text, varied writing styles, and less familiar topics.

Whichever book is right for your reader, Blastoff! Readers are the perfect books to build confidence and encourage a love of reading that will last a lifetime!

This edition first published in 2018 by Bellwether Media, Inc.

No part of this publication may be reproduced in whole or in part without written permission of the publisher. For information regarding permission, write to Bellwether Media, Inc., Attention: Permissions Department, 5357 Penn Avenue South, Minneapolis, MN 55419.

Library of Congress Cataloging-in-Publication Data

Names: Koestler-Grack, Rachel A., 1973- author.
Title: Earth Day / by Rachel Grack.
Description: Minneapolis, MN : Bellwether Media, Inc., 2018. | Series:
    Blastoff! Readers. Celebrating Holidays | Includes bibliographical
    references and index. | Audience: Grades K-3. | Audience: Ages 5-8.
Identifiers: LCCN 2016052750 (print) | LCCN 2016053282 (ebook) | ISBN
    9781626176195 (hardcover : alk. paper) | ISBN 9781681033495 (ebook)
Subjects: LCSH: Earth Day–Juvenile literature. | Environmental
    protection–Juvenile literature. | Environmentalism–Juvenile literature.
Classification: LCC GE195.5 .K64 2018 (print) | LCC GE195.5 (ebook) | DDC
    394.262–dc23
LC record available at https://lccn.loc.gov/2016052750

Editor: Christina Leighton   Designer: Lois Stanfield

Printed in the United States of America, North Mankato, MN.

Table of Contents

Earth Day Is Here!

Families bike and enjoy nature. People clean up trash in neighborhoods.

They plant trees in parks.
It is Earth Day!

What Is Earth Day?

Earth Day is a holiday about caring for the **environment**.

People help keep the air, land, and water clean. They do things that are "**green**."

How to Be Green

Be green by practicing the three Rs every day!

Reduce: turn off lights and water when not in use

Reuse: use lunch boxes and cloth bags instead of paper and plastic

Recycle: separate cans, plastic, glass, and paper from trash

Who Celebrates Earth Day?

Earth Day started in the United States.

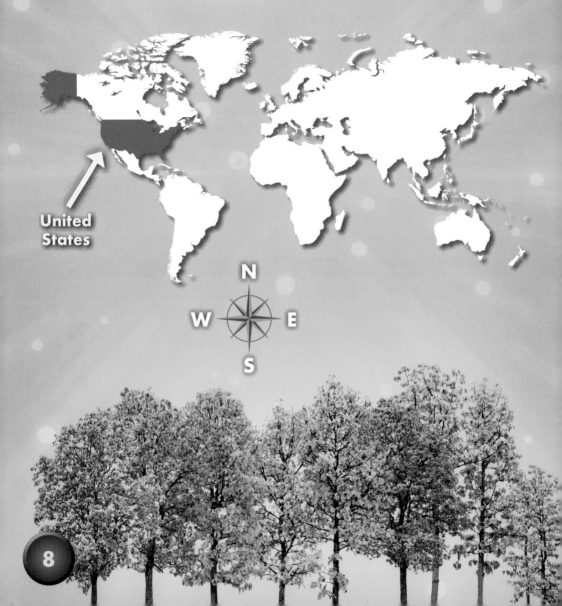

United States

N

W E

S

Today, people all over the world celebrate this holiday. They honor the planet and make the environment cleaner.

Earth Day Beginnings

pollution

Before 1970, there were very few laws about **pollution**. Factories dumped waste into rivers and lakes. They filled the air with harmful smoke.

Endangered animals were not **protected**.

Many Americans wanted people to care about nature. They held the first Earth Day on April 22, 1970.

Earth Day planning, 1970

Earth Day, 1970

It was a success! The day helped to pass laws that protect the environment.

Time to Celebrate

Most countries have
Earth Day every April 22.

Vancouver, Canada

Other countries celebrate on the first day of spring. Some communities do green activities all week!

Earth Day Traditions!

wind turbines making
clean electricity

Earth Day reminds people to save water and **electricity**.

People **donate** or reuse old items. They also teach others how to **recycle**.

People take action on Earth Day. They pick up roadside trash. Some people walk instead of drive. Others plant gardens and trees.

Plant Baby Lettuce

Grow baby lettuce seeds indoors! When the plants need more space, move them outside or to a larger pot.

What You Need:
- cardboard egg carton
- potting soil
- spoon
- baby lettuce seeds
- rimmed baking sheet
- spray bottle with water
- scissors

What You Do:
1. Use the spoon to fill all egg wells with soil.
2. Poke a hole in the soil of each well with your finger.
3. Drop three or four seeds in each well.
4. Cover the seeds with soil.
5. Place the egg carton on a rimmed baking sheet.
6. Spray each well to lightly water the soil.
7. Place the egg carton near a window so that it gets sunlight.
8. Check the soil every day and spray with water if it is dry.
9. After sprouts appear, thin them with scissors so they are about 1 inch apart.
10. Continue keeping the soil slightly wet.
11. Cut and eat the lettuce after about a month when it is 4 inches long!

4

9

Many groups raise money to save wildlife. Families learn about nature at special events.

hawksbill sea turtle

ring-tailed lemurs

People around the world
protect the environment on
Earth Day!

Glossary

donate—to give something away to help people in need

electricity—a form of energy that gives power

endangered—at risk of dying out completely

environment—the surrounding natural conditions that affect the ability to survive

green—related to learning and doing things that care for the environment

pollution—something that is harmful to the air, water, or land

protected—kept something or someone from harm

recycle—to separate cans, plastic, glass, and paper from trash; these items can be made into new things.

To Learn More

AT THE LIBRARY

Cella, Clara. *Earth Day*. Mankato, Minn.: Capstone Press, 2013.

Owings, Lisa. *From Garbage to Compost*. Minneapolis, Minn.: Lerner Publications, 2017.

Ponto, Joanna. *Earth Day*. New York, N.Y.: Enslow Publishing, 2016.

ON THE WEB

Learning more about Earth Day is as easy as 1, 2, 3.

1. Go to www.factsurfer.com.

2. Enter "Earth Day" into the search box.

3. Click the "Surf" button and you will see a list of related web sites.

With factsurfer.com, finding more information is just a click away.

Index

The images in this book are reproduced through the courtesy of: ixpert, front cover (globe), p. 22; Joachim Wendler, front cover (hands); Kzenon, p. 4; wavebreakmedia, pp. 4-5; Andrew Mayovskyy, pp. 6-7; puruan, p. 7 (recycle icon); Doucefleur, p. 8; Joseph Sohm, p. 9; Tatiana Grozetskaya, pp. 10-11; Hung_Chung_Chih, p. 11; AP Images, pp. 12, 13; kali9, p. 14; Sergei Bachlakov, pp. 14-15; WDG Photo, pp. 16-17; JBryson, p. 17; asiseeit, p. 18; Dabchai labchait, p. 19 (top); prachyaloyfar, p. 19 (lower left); andy lane/ Alamy, p. 19 (lower right); Rich Carey, p. 20 (left); Eric Gevaert, p. 20 (right); Syda Productions, pp. 20-21.